Potential² Manifesto

Finding Your Infinite Potential by Living Your Gifts Every Day

Tracy Worley

Potential² Manifesto

Find Your Infinite Potential by Living Your Gifts Every Day

Stop Giving Up Before the End of the Trail

By Tracy A. Worley

Copyright © by Tracy A. Worley
and Red Shoe, LLC
All Rights Reserved

Cover Design: Chris Mendoza
Editor: Gerrie Wall
Photo Credit: Tracy Worley

Potential² Manifesto
Find Your Infinite Potential by Living Your Gifts Every Day

Mount Aeneas, Elevation 7528

The top of Mount Aeneas is in the foreground and less than a mile to go.

My husband and border collies hiked this loop trail September of 2013. This was a day hike with over 2,000 vertical. The beautiful views from the top and the loop are a reminder of when we give up before the end of the trail we give up on our success, dreams, and joy.

Stop Giving Up Before the End of the Trail

Tracy A. Worley

Table of Contents

Part One: Power of Potential
 Without limitation, do you know who you are?

Part Two: What is Potential
 Why finding your Potential^2 is important.

Part Three: Where to Start
 Finding value in you.

Part Four: Potential^2
 Ten steps to your Potential^2.

About the Author

Discover Your Potential^2

Resources and Links
 Connect with P^2 Red Shoe Tribe, go to the website for the tribe link.
 www.RedShoeLLC.com

Part One: Power of Potential

Who are you and why are you here? Before answering this question, I will tell you who I am and why I am here. Through decades of learning from the best mentors and my mistakes, I know my who and why. I wish this for you, too. As I sit here envisioning you reading this *Potential² Manifesto*, I pray you have grace, hope, and courage to discover your potential, purpose and heart's desire in and from life.

Most people use only a small fraction of their ability and rarely strive to reach their potential. A few years ago, my world came crashing down around me without my permission. Within a short period, I found myself divorced and downsized. I had hard choices: To *live* or *die,* or as my friend and mentor, Kary Oberbrunner, teaches, *"be a victim or a victor."* I ask you, when life deals you "lemons'" are you choosing to <u>*live or die*</u>, to be a <u>*victim or a victor*</u>? From my life experiences, I found my Potential² and that is to **gracefully inspire and empower others to achieve their infinite potential**.

Definition: Infinite Potential (Potential²) is growing, learning, and adding value to self and others until we are no longer able to take another breath on this earth.

One way to be *alive* and be a *victor* is to be on a path of knowledge. Knowledge is only powerful when it is applied to be more than you are today. Did you know?

> One-third of high school graduates will never read another book after graduation.
>
> 42% of college graduates will never read another book after graduation.
>
> 32% of the U.S. population has never been in a bookstore.

Most people are willing to settle for average in life, and I hope you are not willing to settle for average!

> ***"To grow, you must be willing to let your present and future to be totally unlike your past. Your history is not your destiny." (Alan Cohen)***

Respond to each of the following statements (yes or no):
- I am *excited* to get up every morning when the alarm goes off.
- I *dream* on a daily basis.

- I *Daily,* read an article(s) or a book.
- I can *easily* say "no" to others' request of my time.
- My daily agenda is filled with people, places, and activities I *enjoy.*
- I can tell people my personal ***values*** without hesitation.

If you answered "no" to any of the above, you are not living up to your potential. Surprised? Take heart and look up; most of us are only living a fraction of our potential. Better yet, keep reading and learn how to start living your Infinite potential; in other words, Potential².

Throughout history we read stories of heroes who are not living out their God-given talents. One story I love to read is that of Samson. Samson's potential was foretold to his mother, "You will become pregnant and give birth to a son, and his hair must never be cut. For he will be dedicated to God as a Nazirite from birth. He will rescue Israel from the Philistines" (Judges 13:5).

Samson's gifts and potential were written before he was conceived. Just as Samson, we too are part of God's plan to live out our gifts and Potential[2]. Samson was given great strength; his strength was sustained by following a few guidelines to not cut hair, touch a dead body, or drink alcohol. We too are able to sustain the strengths of our gifts by proclaiming we are weak and finding strength in God. "My gracious favor is all you need. My power works best in your weakness" (2 Cor. 12:9).

Jesus is not stating we live and work in areas we are weak, but he is telling us to give everything in our strength and faith by sustaining our gifts and living out our Potenial[2]. Samson led a blessed life, yet through freedom of choice he was often in torment by not living fully within his gifts. By the end of his life he became a slave to his enemy where he was humiliated and often brought out into public forums to perform.

Although Samson was blind by the end of his life, he had many hours to think about his life choices of distraction from his gifts. Even though Samson had been far from his gifts and God, his last breath and courageous act was asking God to once again fill him with strength. "Then Samson prayed to the LORD, 'Sovereign LORD, remember me again. O God, please strengthen me one more time so that I may pay back the Philistines for the loss of my eyes.' Then Samson put his hands on the center pillars of the temple and pushed against them with all his might. 'Let me die with the Philistines,' he prayed. And the temple crashed down on the Philistine leaders and all the people.

Samson killed more people when he died than he had during his entire lifetime"(Judges 17:28-30). In his last courageous act with his gift of strength restored, Samson destroyed his enemies living out Potenial[2].

Part Two:
The Essence of Potential

Potential^2 is growing, learning, and adding value to self and others until you no longer are able to take another breath on this earth. Potential^2 is living out the gifts and talents we are given and refining them to live the *fullest life possible*. Fullest life? Your potential carries a life and energy force of its own. When living within your gifts, your potential for joy and success comes naturally and without struggle. This equals your fullest life.

Outside influences, thoughts and emotions hinder your gifts, purpose, passion, and ultimately your potential. Potential^2 is truly your purpose; it is what makes your heart beat faster. Potential^2 makes you smile without thinking. The first step to finding your gifts, talents, purpose, and potential is to devote time and energy to what you love doing. When you spend time in the gifts God has blessed you with, you are creating the genius of your individual self; Potential^2. Here are a few questions to ask yourself and start finding where you are spending time, energy, and gifts.

- 💪 Do you review your daily agenda and identify activities and people who do not "fit" within your Potential^2?
- 💪 Do you have mentor(s) to help find, sharpen and lift your gifts, and hold you accountable?
- 💪 Are you a mentor to others who you can help sharpen, lift, and model accountability to their Potential^2?

"Visioning our plan, gifts, and desires leads us to reach our Potential^2 and the courage to push out of our comfort zone."

Having mentors in life keeps you on track, unstuck, and accountable to Potential^2. I know the word "accountability" may excite you or a little nauseous, but this is the way to living your Potential^2.

In the past one of my mentors, Paul Martinelli, took me to task, by halting my let's get down to-business attitude. While on this call with teammates, Paul had let us know how he was doing. I want to be courteous to my teammates by not asking Paul the same questions, such as "how are you today".

So, when I engaged in conversation, I stated, "Paul, sounds like you are doing well, and you know I am all about business, so here is my first question." Right then Paul halted my thought process and said, "Well let's not get down to business; how is the family? What are you planning for the holiday season? What traditions do you have? What traditions will you start? Where do you envision spending the holiday's five years from now?"

From the first question Paul asked, I was stuck; I could not answer any of the questions. There was painful silence, stuttering, and disbelief; I could not quickly and openly answer personal questions to my friend and mentor. Several of my team members witnessed the awesomeness of the awkward moment. Yes, awkward is awesome, painful accountability awakens us to a new level of creativity and Potential[2]. From this call I knew there was some adjustment in my thought process, potential, and intentionality in my business and personal joy. I tabled this to the next day when my husband and I would be on the cross country skiing trail. This is always a great time for me to meditate, reflect, and let go.

While on the cross country ski trail this is the mantra that came to my mind and I repeated with each pull, push, and slide: live it, breathe it, and vision it. What was I living? Where was I dedicating my breath? What is my vision of personal and professional success? My mind started to clear to a path of Potential[2]. As the path was clearing in my mind and reasons of the barriers and how to push them out of the way, a barrier on the ski trail appeared. There was a dip in the trail. There are two choices to ski the barrier. The first choice is to do a quick hop, skip, and jump over. The second choice, I decided to play it safe by slowing down, slide in and out of the dip.

By playing it safe I got stuck. Literally I was stuck in a snow bank; by my slowing down, both ski tips pushed forward into the snow bank instead of sliding in and out. I was now living a Looney Toon Cartoon with both tips of my skis stuck, the back of the skis sticking out into free space, my torso and face flat into the snow bank; my backside was the only thing my husband could see as it was sticking straight in the air.

The first thought was not how to get unstuck. My first response was pounding a fist on the snow and saying darn you, Paul Martinelli! You see, it was not his fault I was stuck; it was mine by playing it safe on the trail and in life. Just as on the call the day before, I was playing it safe by not living my Potential[2]. Paul's push to the line of intention not only pushed me to a higher level of awareness and creativity but also gave me the title and content of a new book I am working on, *Vision of Grace Stuck in a Snow Bank*.

"Suspend the need to know how and just step up to the line of intention."
(Paul Martinelli)

Are you stopping before you get to the end? Are you stopping before you succeed? Are you suspending success by needing to know everything before you start? Imagine a picture showing two men digging, and, with only five feet to go, one man keeps digging and finds gold. The second man quits and never reaps the reward. I love hiking in the mountains, and the reward at the top. I am given 360 bird's-eye views most people will never experience in their lifetime. Ascending vertical climbs are tough, especially when there are steep elevation gains in the short distance left to the top. Most of the time this feels like a belly crawl. It is easy to give up, not get dirty, not get a scrape or bruise. What keeps me going? The sweet reward of success, striving, sweating, and reaching my Potential^2 to succeed to the top!

> ## *"Stop giving up on your Potential^2 by giving up too soon!"*

Part Three: Where to Start

Another friend and mentor, John Maxwell, states, "Do everything in your power to grow yourself and create the right environment to grow." Is your current environment hindering your ability to find your purpose and Potential[2]? John gives us a check list to find out where you are, ask if these characteristics fit you:

- Others are ahead of me
- I wake up excited
- I am continually challenged
- Failure is not my enemy
- My focus is forward
- Others around me are growing
- The atmosphere is affirming
- People desire change
- I am often out of my comfort zone
- Growth is modeled and expected

Others are ahead of me? This is where humility of our hearts comes to play. To go farther and to places we have never been, we must look to and for those who are ahead of us. Learning from their experienced wisdom is the fastest way to success.

> *"Everyone is composed of a few themes."* (C.S. Lewis)

The second step is to start leading yourself from where you are right now! Right now where you are sitting, wiggle in your seat a bit and feel your mind and body connect. From your body and mind connection sitting in your chair, start leading yourself. Leading yourself means *not waiting for someone* else to start or do it for you; you are responsible for yourself! So, from here lead yourself into the purpose and Potential[2] you deserve, desire, and most importantly, dream about. Remember, we can all exceed in what we believe we "cannot" do. So start doing and, even if you fail, it is a start toward finding your future and Potential[2]. Someone once stated, "We are responsible for creating the future we want or enduring the future we get." Basically, you must create a future from your purpose and gifts, and not ask permission; otherwise you give others "veto power" over your Potential[2].

DO NOT ASK FOR PERMSSION ~ STATE YOUR PURPOSE AND MOVE FORWARD

The third step forward is to outline your personal values (Top4 worksheet). Knowing your individual values gives you boundaries to be authentic to yourself and protect your gifts and Potential[2]. I believe we live within two sets of values.

> Big V: These are societal values, such as do not murder, cheat, steal, speed, lie, etc.
> Little v: These are our personal values, such as family, career, health, faith, education, etc.

There are other values you may also follow, such as those of an organization, volunteer group, or church you belong to. I have walked many participants through this exercise, and they find once they have identified their Top4, creation of authentic boundaries and the freedom to say "no" come with ease.

At the end of this manifesto, I have included where you can start your Top4 and begin moving forward into your Potential[2].

Part Four: Potential^2

We all experience peaks and valleys in our lives. It doesn't matter where we have been in the past or where we find ourselves now. Growth can come from a positive attitude and the willingness to challenge our self-beliefs to create a purposeful life into our Potential^2. We move forward trusting our personal wisdom through imagination and dreams.

"Imagination is more important than knowledge." (Albert Einstein)

"A child is born with no self-image. Every idea, opinion, feeling, attitude, or value is learned from childhood experience. Everything you are today is the result of an idea or impression you accepted as true. When you believe something to be true, it becomes true for you." (Ron McIntosh).

What does this statement say to you? For me this statement breathes life into allowing no limitations when living within our God-given talents and Potential^2.

First steps to your Potential^2

- Do not settle for average.
- Create the future you want (stop giving up).
- Find your gifts & talents (what are you most passionate about or where do you excel).
- Focus on Potential^2 and not outside influences.
- Review daily agenda (Top4).
- Find and stay connected to mentor(s).
- Be uncomfortable every day.
- Create an environment for growth.
- Lead yourself (step up to the line of intention).
- Identify your Top4 Values (boundaries).

Every day, live your Potential^2 by growing, learning, and adding value to self and others. You were born without limitations. Look UP and OUT, my FRIENDS!

Where are you stopping before the end of the trail?

Connect with Tracy to find your Potential^2 trail.

About: Tracy Worley

Tracy gracefully inspires and empowers people to their Infinite Potential.

Tracy Worley is America's leading grace coach, international key-note speaker, trainer, syndicated radio host, author, potential seeker, strategist and CEO of three values leadership based organizations.

She works with business executives, entrepreneurs, and leaders world-wide to develop their potential, tailor employee engagement modules, and turn up the volume on individuals and organizations potential personally and professionally.

Tracy knows firsthand about what it takes to find your potential. Individuals and organizations have unique cultures, stories, and rhythm – Tracy's innovative style knows how to make it work. With a background in business management, business communication, relationship building, project management, and life's drama, Tracy found herself running a multi-million dollar organization at the age of 25.

Tracy knows from life experience the ups and downs of colossal failure and the elation of success beyond imagination. Success builds from a relationship of loving self and others; communication is the secret.

These gifts give Tracy the ability to strategize with clarity where you are, where you want to be, and how to get there. Tracy's expertise: training highly successful people to lead with authenticity to the desired success her client's desire and deserve.

Tracy lives in Missoula with her husband Tim and son Steven; completing a rounded circle of ying-and-yang of two outdoor book nerds. Tracy's administrative staff share in all of the Red Shoe success, Jill and Kimber (2 Border Collies).

Connect with P² Red Shoe Tribe

Twitter

Facebook

Website

LinkedIN

Go to **www.RedShoeLLC.com** for the links.

Discover Your Potenial²

In this free training you will learn and create:
- Your Top4 Personal Values
- Personal and Professional Mission Statement
- Daily Agenda Review and Tools

And so much more. . . just by saying YES to your Potential²

Yep, I believe in you so much I am offering free training to get your started toward the joyful success you desire and deserve.

Go to **www.RedShoeLLC** to find downloads to the worksheets. Work at your own pace or ask for a free 45 minute consultation to launch your P².

Join the P² Tribe

To find out more about how you can get involved in *P² Tribe* and how you can accelerate your growth personally and professionally, go to **www.RedShoeLLC.com**.

Share This Manifesto

You are welcome to share this manifesto with anyone and everyone. There is an eBook version too.

I only ask that you do not sell or change it in any way.

Here are some ways to share:
Twitter | Facebook | Comments